The Simplicity of Spiritual Enlightenment

What to know, and do, to quickly
awaken to conscious awareness
of the truth of your real nature
in relationship with God

ROY EUGENE DAVIS

CSA Press / Lakemont, Georgia

copyright© 2004 by Roy Eugene Davis

ISBN 0-87707-291-4

CSA Press
Post Office Box 7
Lakemont, Georgia 30552-0001

Telephone: 706-782-4723
Fax: 706-782-4560
e-mail: csainc@csa-davis.org
web site: www.csa-davis.org

CSA Press is the publishing department of
Center for Spiritual Awareness

PRINTED IN THE UNITED STATES OF AMERICA

Open your mind and your heart (the true essence of your being) to the Infinite.

Reverently acknowledge God however God is real to you, around and within you.

Reverently acknowledge the saints and sages of all enlightenment traditions.

Reverently acknowledge the innate, divine nature of every person.

Reverently acknowledge the truth of your innermost level of being, knowing that all knowledge of the unbounded field of Infinite Consciousness is within you.

May you be permanently established in conscious realization of your relationship with the Infinite.

May you be steadfast on your meaningful spiritual path as it is revealed to you.

May everyone be spiritually enlightened.

Other Books By The Author
Published by CSA Press

Satisfying Our Innate Desire to Know God

A Master Guide to Meditation

The Science of God-Realization

The Path of Light
Kriya Yoga and Patanjali's yoga-sutras

Seven Lessons in Conscious Living
Guidelines to Kriya Yoga Practice

The Eternal Way
The Inner Meaning of the Bhagavad Gita

An Easy Guide to Ayurveda

Una Guía Maestra para la Meditación
A Master Guide to Meditation (Spanish edition)

Mr. Davis books are also published in India by:
Motilal Banarsidass
40 U.A., Bungalow Road, Jawahar Nagar
Delhi 110 007
Tel: 391-1985 Fax: 011-393-0689
e-mail: mlbd@vsnl.com   Web site: www.mlbd.com

And at Motilal Banarsidass bookstores in:
Varanasi, Patna, Kolkata, Chennai, Bangalore,
Pune, and Mumbai.

INTRODUCTION

Our awakening through the stages of spiritual growth can be slow, moderate, fast, or rapid in accord with our aspiration and right endeavors.

How your spiritual growth can be quickened is explained in the following pages. For optimum results, read the text several times and apply what you learn.

It is your destiny to be spiritually enlightened. At the innermost level of your being you are now whole, serene, and knowledgeable. Assume this to be true and let it be actualized.

Roy Eugene Davis

Lakemont, Georgia
May 2004

Publisher's Note

Chapters two and three were previously published as articles and have been revised by the author.

Contents

Introduction
— 5 —

Word Meanings to Know
— 8 —

Chapter One
The Simplicity of Spiritual Enlightenment
— 9 —

Chapter Two
The Importance of Total Commitment
to the Spiritual Path
— 17 —

Chapter Three
Make Your Life Worthwhile
— 24 —

Chapter Four
Answers to Questions
— 34 —

Supplements
The Categories of Cosmic Manifestation *14*
How to Practice Superconscious Meditation *16*

Word Meanings to Know

clarify To make clear or pure.

contemplation Attentive examination of a thing or concept with alert expectation of discovery.

God The one Reality. The absolute aspect is pure existence-being. The expressive aspect has attributes which emanate and sustain universes.

grace Divine assistance freely, effortlessly provided when we are receptive to it.

ego The illusional perception of self-identity.

enlighten To provide spiritual insight, knowledge.

meditation Introspective contemplation practiced to calm the mind and clarify awareness.

metaphysics The systematic, orderly investigation of first principles of ultimate reality, the nature of being, and cosmology.

prayer Reverent invocation of divine influence.

Self Our essence as a unit of pure Consciousness. Souls are units with an illusional sense of self.

simple Easy, not complicated or difficult.

subliminal Below the threshold of our conscious perception.

realization Flawless perception with knowledge of what is perceived. When we awaken from the illusional sense of self, we are Self-realized. When we apprehend the reality of God, we are God-realized.

ONE

The Simplicity of Spiritual Enlightenment

An enlivening Power is nurturing the universe and we can learn to cooperate with It.

To be enlightened about something is to have knowledge of it. To be *spiritually enlightened* is to have flawless knowledge of our true nature, the reality of God, and the processes of life.

Spiritual growth doesn't have to be difficult. It is too often believed that discovering the truth about our essence of being and our relationship with God requires years of arduous endeavor and a need to struggle to overcome a great variety of obstacles and troublesome circumstances.

To be spiritually enlightened:

- Fervently aspire to be fully, spiritually awake.
- Acquire accurate knowledge of your true nature and God.
- Acquire knowledge of what to do to allow your innate potential to be actualized—and apply it.

Many "truth seekers" experience unnecessary difficulties and occasional or frequent episodes of frustration and despair because they do not yet have an intellectual understanding of their essential nature, the reality of God, and what they hope to accomplish and how to do it. While their intentions may be good, they are confused. Their thoughts and behaviors are determined by egocentric attitudes, subliminal urges, acquired cultural beliefs, irrational choices, or the self-centered behaviors and flawed opinions of spiritually unaware people with whom they relate or admire or whose approval they desire to have.

You can know *about* God by learning from others who are already God-knowledgable. You can *know* God by improving your intellectual and intuitive powers and clarifying your mind and awareness until your innate knowledge emerges and blossoms into wisdom.

That which is commonly referred to as God (word origin: Old German, "the highest good") has a transcendent (beyond relative, objective phenomena) aspect and a modified aspect with characteristics. The transcendent aspect cannot be fully comprehended by the mind or intellect; it can be experienced because we are units of it. The modified aspect can be related to and its attributes and actions comprehended.

Spiritual enlightenment is not a goal to be achieved, nor is it the effect of any cause. It is actualized (real in fact) when we awaken to the truth of what we are and our relationship with God. Spiritual awakening is usually gradual, with partial insights preceding comprehensive discoveries. It can also occur instantaneously. One is advised to patiently, skillfully adhere to a course of useful study and spiritual practice while being attentive to the possibility of sudden awakening that can occur.

To be *patient* is to be mentally and emotionally calm while performing duties and choosing and accomplishing purposes which are of value. To be *skillful* is to be proficient in thought and deed. To *adhere* is to persist without wavering. Useful *study* enables helpful knowledge to be acquired. Useful *spiritual practice* prepares us to awaken to Self- and God-knowledge.

Satori is the Japanese word for meaningful insight which may be partial, as glimpses of what is true, or sudden and complete. Mental calmness, orderly living, metaphysical study, and meditation practiced to clarify awareness can make us receptive to meaningful insights.

Among yogis, the Sanskrit word *samadhi* is used to describe superconscious states that can be cultivated to purify the mind and awareness. Preliminary samadhi states may be mixed with thoughts and moods. Pure states are devoid of thoughts and emotions. Both are preliminary to transcendence during which direct perception of ultimate Reality is realized.

Pure superconsciousness is experienced when the meditator's emotions are settled, the mind is calm, thoughts cease, and subliminal influences are dormant. So long as the mind is somewhat restless or subliminal influences are not yet dormant, pure samadhi cannot prevail even though a fleeting, pure superconscious state may sometimes occur.

Meditative superconsciousness is a completely internalized state during which attention and vital forces are withdrawn from environmental conditions, the senses, and the mind, and the meditator remains conscious and attentive to what is being experienced and observed. The final realization is freedom from identification with any influences which might blur or modify one's awareness.

When flawless realization is unwavering, one clearly discerns the reality of pure consciousness as existence-being and that all relative phenomena has no independent or permanent basis. With awareness returned to its Source, one who is spiritually enlightened discerns that so-called spiritual and material realities are manifestations of one Reality and is able to freely function and express in accord with that knowledge without again falling back into ordinary states of awareness.

Thus permanently spiritually enlightened, a person who lives effectively with understanding is liberated from the troubles that are common to people whose awareness is blurred. Although some effects of past unwise actions may still occur, the enlightened person does not suffer, nor does anything that occurs mar or diminish their Self- and God-realization. In the course of time, influences of subconscious conditionings which were once troublesome, and residues of latent unwise desires, are weakened and neutralized by the superior influences of the superconscious state that prevails. Liberation of consciousness is then realized.

Spontaneous Self-realization occurs when the illusional sense of self is transcended.

Spiritual enlightenment should not be thought of as a goal to be achieved during or after transition from the body, but as a present-time possibility in your current incarnation. Neither should it be thought of as a reward for good behavior. There are millions of "good" people in the world whose awareness is ordinary and for whom the urge to be spiritually aware is not yet compelling. All souls will eventually aspire to spiritual growth that culminates in liberation of consciousness and will have their awareness restored to its original purity.

We were expressed as individualized units of the one field of pure Consciousness because of its interactions with the primordial field of nature (a projected vibration of its power that manifests time, space, and fine cosmic forces from which universes are emanated).

When units are individualized, they become attracted to the field of primordial nature or are projected into it by the power that emanates it and their awareness is blurred. A covering of fine material substance is then attracted by the unit which enables it to have a degree of intellectual discrimination. A further covering of mental substance is attracted that processes perceptions and concepts (the mind). These coverings, with a soul's innate awareness and an illusional sense of self, while somewhat confining, enable it to relate to and function in the material realm.

The Categories and Sequential Processes of Cosmic Manifestation

The Field of Absolute (pure) Consciousness

Expressive Aspect of God With Attributes That Make Possible Cosmic Manifestation

Primordial Nature
The vibration of the power of Consciousness, space, time, and fine cosmic forces. Souls are individualized by interactions of supreme Consciousness with primordial nature.

Cosmic Mind
The one mind of which our minds are units. Responsive to our mental states and thoughts, it produces corresponding events and circumstances.

Subtle Essences of the Five Senses
Of smell, taste, touch, sight, and hearing.

Subtle Essences of the Five Modes of Action
Assimilation, elimination, reproduction, mobility, and dexterity.

Subtle Essences of the Five Elements
Ether (space with cosmic forces), air, fire, water, earth or matter.

Gross Manifestation of the Essences of the Five Elements in and as the physical world.

When a soul is attracted to a gross material realm, it is provided with a physical body. When it is mostly identified with a mind, body, and environmental conditions, perception of its true nature is flawed.

The two direct ways to become aware of your true nature are by:

- Using your intellect and intuition to discern the difference between yourself as the observer and ordinary states of awareness. When you know what you are not, you can know what you are.
- Regular practice of meditation to the stage of superconsciousness.

Meditation that is practiced to elicit pleasant moods or to experience a degree of mental or emotional peace, while useful for managing stress, does not always result in spiritual growth or illumination of consciousness.

Affirm With Conviction
I know that I am an immortal, spiritual being abiding in the wholeness of God.

How to Practice Superconscious Meditation

Meditate in a quiet environment early in the morning or whenever you prefer to do it.

1. Sit upright. Breathe deeply two or three times. Relax. Put your attention in the front and upper region of your brain. If you pray to invoke an awareness of God's presence, do it now.

2. Calmly sit, waiting and observing as your mind becomes calm.

3. If your attention wanders or thoughts persist, use a meditation technique to focus your attention. You may mentally repeat a chosen word such as "God" or "peace" until thoughts are stilled, then disregard the mantra and continue to sit in the silence.

4. When your awareness is clear, abide in that superconscious state for a while.

5. Endeavor to maintain your calm, clear state of awareness after meditation.

Practice 20 to 30 minutes once or twice a day until you can meditate easily. Sit longer if you choose to do so.

TWO

The Importance of Total Commitment to the Spiritual Path

Don't go only half of the way, three quarters of the way, or almost to the end and then quit. Go all the way in this incarnation. – *Paramahansa Yogananda (1893 – 1952)*

Many truth seekers tell me they are not satisfied with their progress on the spiritual path and want to know what to do to more obviously actualize their innate potential.

Spiritual growth is the spontaneous emergence of divine qualities that occurs when conditions which formerly confined them are absent.

Some of the obstacles to spiritual growth are restlessness, confusion, emotional unrest, doubt, attachment to false beliefs, flawed perception of what is observed, neurotic behaviors, addictions, laziness, and an unrefined nervous system or undeveloped brain. Remove all obstacles by cultivating mental calmness, emotional peace, rational thinking, powers of discernment, self-discipline, enthusiasm and purposefulness, good health habits, and skillful meditation practice.

The primary obstacle to overcome is the false perception of self which confines awareness and causes us to think and feel that we are mortal beings. Rational thinking and insights that can occur when meditating superconsciously enable us to realize our inherent, changeless essence and to know our oneness with God.

Common Mistakes to Avoid

Until Self- and God-realization is permanent, a mistaken sense of self may incline us to think or behave as impelled by habit or irrational ideas that arise in the mind.

The following mistakes should be avoided:

- *Reluctance to make a resolute commitment to the spiritual path.*

If you really want to be Self-and God-realized, decide to do it as soon as possible. Immediately begin to do what can be done to allow your innate divine qualities to be actualized. Unwavering commitment will make it easier for you to do what is necessary to accomplish your aims.

- *Procrastination.*

Establish your priorities and cheerfully do what is important or necessary without delay.

- *Allowing moods, whims, or opinions of others to determine your thoughts or actions.*

Acquire the knowledge you need to accomplish purposes of value and make rational decisions about what you will do. You are responsible for how you live and for the choices you make and their results. Be Self-determined. Live from the core essence of your being rather than at the surface of your awareness where you might be too easily influenced by moods, random thoughts, or external circumstances.

• *Failure to wisely use available time, energy, and abilities.*

Prioritize the use of your available time and efficiently do the most important things first. Don't deplete vital forces by excessive talking, worry, unwholesome habits, or depriving your body and mind of necessary rest. Wisely use your functional skills by concentrating on goals and purposes which are of value to you.

• *Superficial interest in spirituality.*

Be sincerely intent on knowing the truth about your Self, God, and mundane and metaphysical (beyond the physical) laws of cause and effect. Be curious about the possibilities of discovering the real meaning of your life and how to acquire the understanding that will enable you to live effectively as you awaken through the stages of spiritual growth.

• *Superficial application of knowledge.*

Skillfully use the knowledge you now have to verify it. Think constructively. Be a possibility-thinker. Use imagination creatively. Learn how states of awareness and mental states attract a corresponding response from Universal Mind. You will then understand why it is important for you to be responsible for maintaining a clear state of awareness and wisely choosing your thoughts, moods, and actions. If your existing circumstances are not ideal, admit that they conform to your states of awareness, mental and emotional states, choices, decisions, and actions. To change existing conditions, change your state of awareness, mental and emotional states, and actions. You can choose to be the master of your fate (the conditions that you cause, or allow, to manifest or persist).

- *Reading, talking about, or using spiritual practices which are not useful or appropriate for your personal needs.*

Doing these things is a waste of time and will only further confuse your mind, disturb your emotions, complicate your life, and thwart or delay your spiritual progress. Discover and use the spiritual practices that will satisfy your real needs and are compatible with your mental and physical characteristics.

The reliable means by which authentic spiritual growth can be nurtured are already known:

1. Cultivate compassion, truthfulness, honesty, conservation and wise use of vital forces while performing duties without strong attachment to your actions or their results.

2. Maintain good health habits. Cultivate soul contentment in all circumstances. Nurture your psychological well-being. Contemplate your true nature as pure consciousness and the reality of God until you discern what is true. See through and rise

above the illusional sense of selfhood.

3. Practice superconscious meditation until you are firmly established in Self- and God-realization and your awareness is free from all false beliefs and illusions.

- *Preoccupation with philosophical theories or new or "advanced" meditation techniques.*

Study what enlightened people have said rather than be involved with theoretical speculation. When you acquire new information, examine it until it is comprehended.

After meditation techniques are learned, they should be diligently used. Meditation techniques are "tools" to be used to calm the mind and clarify awareness. Prayer, use of a mantra (a word or word-phrase used to focus attention), pranayama practiced to harmonize flows of the body's vital forces, and other procedures can be helpful.

- *Excessive or nonuseful social interaction.*

Appropriate, wholesome social interaction can be enjoyable and mutually beneficial. Excessive social interaction may distract you from your major purposes and deplete your energies. When possible, choose to associate with others who are high-minded, rather than with persons who are pessimistic or emotionally dependent. When interacting with others who are self-centered or materialistic, be appropriate while soul-centered and peaceful.

- *Failure to acquire sufficient useful, accurate secu-*

lar and metaphysical knowledge.

Acquiring useful knowledge enables you to live more effectively, and the learning process exercises your mind and improves the capacity of your brain to process information. People who continue to learn tend to remain mentally alert as they become older.

• *Indulging in fantasy.*

Imagining possible circumstances is useful. To allow imagination to be uncontrolled is not useful. Individuals who habitually allow their attention to wander and the mind to be flooded with unreal ideas usually do so because they are not happy or fulfilled and are unwilling to confront the facts of life. A truth seeker should always be realistic and rational. If you are inclined to fantasize, cultivate a dynamic will to live and to actualize your innate potential. Plan and immediately implement constructive goals and projects.

Concentrate on doing what is important for your highest good and the good of others.

The positive results of your commitment to the spiritual path will be:

- Enhanced intellectual and intuitive powers.
- Psychological transformation.
- Greatly improved functional abilities.
- Orderly emergence of innate knowledge.
- Rational thinking and improved powers of creative imagination.
- Progressive clarification of awareness.

- Cosmic consciousness.
- Self-realization.
- God-realization.
- Liberation of consciousness.

The fulfillment you aspire to have is available to you now and can be experienced by accepting it. Go deep into the essence of your being. There, you will discover the truth about yourself and the reality of God.

Affirm With Conviction
I am totally committed to the spiritual path
and will persist with diligent right endeavor
until I am fully Self- and God-realized.

This is the way to remove sorrow and misfortune: right views, right aspiration, right speech, right conduct, right livelihood, right endeavor, right mindfulness, and right contemplation. – *Buddhist teaching*

THREE

Make Your Life Worthwhile

One of the most frequent questions I am asked is, "How can I discover my right place in life and know without any doubts my major purposes?"

Although the ultimate purpose in life for one who is not spiritually enlightened is to awaken to that stage, people who ask the question usually want to know what will be of value for them on a day-to-day basis. If you do not yet feel that your life is worthwhile:

- Pray about it, then be still and observe your thoughts and feelings. Write the thoughts and feelings that arise. If insight with a sense of certainty does not occur, be patient.
- Ask: If I had the freedom, skills, and resources to do what I want to do, what would I do? Write the response.
- If your purpose is well-defined, go forward. If knowledge or skills are needed, acquire knowledge and skills.
- If your purposes are not yet known, be receptive to the promptings of your innate intelligence and what seem to be useful opportunities that life will present from time to time.
- Remain cheerful and optimistic.

Writing your inspired thoughts and plans is important because you may forget the ideas that seemed insightful or the plans you thought might be useful to implement.

A few years ago, managers of a large business were surveyed about their goal-setting practices. It was found that 23% had no specific goals; 67% had minor goals but did not write them; only 10% had long-term goals. Of those with long-term goals, only one person in three wrote a clearly defined plan. The managers with specific goals achieved them 44% percent of the time. Those with written goals had an achievement record of 89%. Purposeful, goal-oriented people expect to be successful, act effectively, and their hopes and endeavors usually produce desired results.

There are several reasons why clearly defined goals enable us to succeed:

- Goals that are vividly imagined, and believed to be possible to achieve, elicit thoughts, plans, and actions that are decisive and productive.
- We are inclined to concentrate on matters considered to be essential and easily disregard those which are not.
- We are more likely to have a well-ordered lifestyle because of being forward-looking and enthusiastic, and our choices in regard to diet, exercise, rest, continuing education, spiritual practices, and socializing are usually more supportive of our long-range goals.

- Our habitual states of awareness and mental states interact with and attract a corresponding response from Universal Mind.

Make your life truly worthwhile by choosing to be responsible for your states of awareness and mental and emotional states.

If unwanted or challenging events occur, don't allow them to disturb your inner peace. When circumstances or relationships are troublesome or distracting, remain calm and make better choices. Cultivate soul-centered awareness at all times regardless of what occurs around you.

Ask for What You Need or Want

What you need, you deserve to have, and your worthy desires should be fulfilled. When you know your relationship with the Infinite, you know this to be true. When you think and feel as though you are an ordinary person, you may be confused. You may think that God may be denying you the security you need or the fulfillment you desire as punishment for past wrong behaviors, or to teach you a lesson. God neither rewards nor punishes; your experiences correspond to your own states of awareness and actions.

Don't believe that subconscious conditionings acquired because of your past thoughts, feelings, and behaviors must determine your experiences or that nothing can be done to improve your life. While subliminal influences can be compelling, you can choose not to be controlled by them. By being soul-centered, subconscious conditionings are weakened and eliminated.

What are your needs? What do you want to experience or have? Perhaps your needs haven't been satisfied or your desires have not been fulfilled because you haven't asked for what you need or want—or haven't asked correctly.

What you ask for can be provided for you. Discriminate between needs and whims, and between desires that can enhance your life when fulfilled and those that may not.

Ask with confidence. Don't beg, or ask for "just enough to enable you to survive" or "make possible a modest degree of fulfillment." You are an immortal spiritual being. Think, feel, and act like what you really are—from the core of your being rather than as an egocentric, personality oriented person. Affirm and acknowledge that which you can imagine as being possible for you to have or experience.

Relate to God however you perceive God to be:

- If you imagine God as an omnipresent being with whom you can relate and who can respond to your prayers, pray to that concept of God.
- If you imagine God as an omnipotent presence, pray to and relate to that.
- If you are aware of abiding in the wholeness of God, acknowledge that it is expressing as, in, and around you in divine order. Cultivate the feeling, knowing, and conviction that you are always in

your "right place" in the universe and that abundant resources and supportive events, circumstances, and relationships for your highest good are spontaneously provided.

Your asking can be silent and mental or you can audibly talk to God as you imagine or know God to be. Talk with God directly. Be specific. Ask for what you need or want until your conviction of having it is strong and unwavering.

If talking with God is a new experience for you, experiment. You will discover that talking with God organizes your thoughts and enables you to more easily determine what is important for your wellbeing. Imagine (or acknowledge) the reality of God where you are. Speak out loud: "God, this is my situation," and go on from there. Describe your circumstances and your real needs. Define your desires and explain why you want them fulfilled. If you have fears or conflicts, or feelings of guilt, insecurity, or incompetence, declare them. If you have bad habits you want to renounce or have good behaviors you want to demonstrate, say so. Reveal everything. Keep talking until you have nothing more to say, then be quiet.

Although God already knows your needs and the desires of your heart, talking with God will help you to be more God-aware and insightful.

Talk with God privately, when you are alone. If at first you feel uncomfortable doing it (or even somewhat foolish), do it anyway. You will soon discover that talking with God is a pleasant and satisfying, beneficial experience.

> Before reading any further, pause for
> a few minutes and talk with God.

Look for What You Need or Want

Be observant. Look beyond conditions that are not compatible with your ideals and aspirations. Imagine what can be possible for you. Mentally "see" it. At the core of your being, acknowledge it and accept it. What seem to be opportunities that may enable you to have your needs satisfied and life-enhancing desires fulfilled, investigate to find out whether or not they can be helpful.

Helpful ideas can sometimes be acquired from what other people say or what you read. Helpful ideas will also spontaneously rise to the surface of your awareness. As you remain alert and attentive, you will discover that you intuitively make good choices and perform right actions. It will become more evident that the universe is supportive of you to the extent of your receptivity and responsiveness. You will be more cosmic conscious. You will intuitively perceive your world as a manifestation of cosmic forces. Your former illusional concepts about God, yourself, and the universe will dissolve. You will realize that there is no separation between God and the material realm in which you abide.

Persist with unwavering faith. Refuse to be unhappy or to indulge in moods. Be cheerful and intentional. Don't allow "bad" news about events that occur in your community or elsewhere in the world to cause you to be fearful, anxious, or depressed. External circumstances are transitory. Be anchored in *that* which does not change.

After an interlude of prayer and meditation, and at all other times, know that you are in harmonious accord with the rhythms of life. Know that what you need is now available to you and that your constructive desires are being fulfilled. Have confident belief (absolute, pure conviction) that your needs are being satisfied and your desires are being fulfilled. Be patient when patience is necessary. Decisively perform actions that will produce the desired results when such actions are necessary.

The Benefits of Orderly Living

Organize your life and be spiritually aware, mentally competent, emotionally balanced and mature, healthy, effectively functional in the accomplishment of worthwhile endeavors, and in harmonious accord with others with whom you relate. A simple (uncomplicated) lifestyle in accord with nature's laws will contribute to your well-being as you successfully accomplish your purposes. Remember that a healthy, long life will enable you to learn what you need to learn, do what you need or want to do, and accomplish your ultimate purpose—to be Self- and God-realized in your present incarnation.

- Eat, sleep, exercise, perform personal duties, and

attend to the needs of others as necessary on a regular schedule. Decide how much time, energy, or material resources to use for these activities.
- When possible, avoid distractions.
- Avoid compulsive or nonuseful expenditure of money. Cultivate a prosperity consciousness: of having what you need when you need it and being able to freely do what you want or need to do. Permanent prosperity will be experienced when the spiritual, mental, emotional, physical, and environmental aspects of your life are harmoniously integrated.
- Conserve your vital forces by avoiding useless, superficial talk, purposeless actions, worry, and stress. You will be healthier, better able to think rationally and make right choices, have improved powers of concentration, and be more spiritually aware.

Review your routine occasionally and modify or improve it when necessary. Experiment until you discover the routine that produces the best results; stay with it until you need to change it. Regular practice will provide useful experience.

Avoid thinking or saying that you cannot meditate. Pray or practice a meditation technique to involve your attention. Fervently aspire to be Self- and God-realized. Don't just sit, feeling helpless or worrying about whether or not you can meditate effectively. Sit until you experience an adjustment of viewpoint that removes your attention and awareness from those conditions. Sit until you experience a superconscious state, during which your awareness is serene and clear. In the early stages, superconsciousness may be mixed with weak thoughts and mild emotions. As you continue to sit and observe, your mind will become peaceful and emotions will be calm.

Contemplate the essence of your being as it is: pure consciousness. Contemplate the reality of God. Surrender to your innate impulse to have your awareness restored to its original purity. When you are surrendered, personal endeavor is neither necessary nor useful because superconscious realizations unfold spontaneously.

Meditative concentration may occasionally be interrupted. Subliminal impulses which are not dormant may cause wavelike movements in the mind. Thoughts may again emerge. Visions or other fantasies may be experienced which should be disregarded. Aspire only to perceive what is permanently real, avoiding fascination with meditative perceptions or sensations. Thoughts and sensations are only relatively real; they are not the ultimate reality.

What to Do When You Have Doubts About What You Believe or Experience

As you awaken through the stages of spiritual growth and continue to learn, it is normal to occasionally be uncertain about some beliefs or experiences that you have had. Inquire:

- Are they valid or true?
- Are they reliable?
- Are they are of value?
- Is my spiritual path the right one for me?
- Am I making the progress I desire to make?

Examine your beliefs and experiences in the light of reason and intuition. Be willing to make new discoveries rather than cling to beliefs and behaviors that are no longer of value to you. The basic philosophical truths do not change, but your understanding of them will improve. If you are certain that your spiritual path is right for you but you are not making the progress you desire and deserve to make, practice with renewed interest. Courageously live up to your highest potential.

Affirm With Conviction
With conscious intention I wisely think
and live to make my life worthwhile.

At fifteen, my mind was inclined toward learning; at thirty, I stood firm; at forty, my mind was free from delusions; at fifty, I understood the will of God; at sixty, my ears were receptive to truth; at seventy, I could follow the promptings of my heart without overstepping the boundaries of right. – *Confucius (551 – 479 B.C.E.)*

FOUR

Answers to Questions

Superior to the senses is the mind; superior to the mind is the intellect; superior to the intellect is the Self [true essence of being]. – *Bhagavad Gita 3:42*

What is the difference between ordinary states of awareness and superconsciousness?

Ordinary states of awareness are confined by a mistaken sense of self, modified mental states, emotional unrest, and erroneous ideas that one may believe to be true.

Superconsciousness (*super*, above) is superior to ordinary waking states, sleep, and dreams. It is the natural state of being that prevails when we remove our attention from the characteristics of ordinary awareness.

Describe what is experienced as one awakens through the stages of spiritual growth.

1. We are aware of troublesome subconscious influences, limiting mental attitudes, erroneous beliefs, and faulty behaviors to avoid to allow further spiritual awakening to naturally occur. Insight and fervent aspiration makes possible wise, concentrated constructive endeavor.

2. Subconscious conditionings which have the

potential to contribute to pain or misfortune are weakened or neutralized and can no longer cause suffering or misfortune.

3. Our refined states of consciousness can easily be discerned and examined.

4. Our relationship to the mind and internal and external conditions is comprehended.

5. Subliminal influences no longer cause changes in our awareness and Self-realization spontaneously occurs.

6. The reality of God is comprehended.

7. The mind is fully illumined, consciousness is liberated, and we abide in constant realization of pure being.

I sincerely want to be spiritually enlightened. Do I need a guru (teacher) to guide and assist me?

Although the wise guidance of someone who is spiritually awake and knowledgeable can be helpful, it is not always available. If you have such a relationship, nurture it and do your best to be a competent disciple (learner). If you do not have a spiritually awake, knowledgeable teacher, learn from other reliable sources, live in accord with your ideals, meditate skillfully, and open your mind and heart (being) to the Infinite. Your innate urge to be fully awake will culminate in spiritual enlightenment. The impulses of God's grace will support and provide for you all that is needed for your highest good. Always remember that wherever you are and whatever you do, you abide in the wholeness of God.

I like to pray when I begin to meditate. What is a good way to do this?

Prayer is a request for divine assistance. Sit quietly, Self-aware, and feel that you abide in God. Verbally, or mentally, ask for God's help as you aspire to be Self- and God-realized. Aspire to awaken to a clear state of awareness.

As the mind becomes calm and your breathing becomes slow and refined, notice that thoughts become more subtle and less forceful. Disregard thoughts and focus your attention on what you want to experience. Surrender to the meditation process that naturally occurs until you are aware of being established in a calm, clear state. Rest there for a while in the deep silence.

While I am intent on my spiritual path, I am also concerned about the welfare of others. How can I help them to be spiritually aware and fulfilled?

Attend to your right living regimens, studies, and spiritual practices while wishing for the highest good for everyone. Your awareness of your true nature and God will blend with and elevate the collective consciousness of others in this and other realms. Because souls are units of one supreme Consciousness, the enlightened consciousness of one soul benefits all souls.

When someone indicates a sincere interest in spirituality, give them a helpful book and allow them to make their own choices. Demonstrate compassion for others while maintaining your own Self- and God-awareness.

At the conclusion of your meditation practice session, established in awareness of wholeness, acknowledge the divine nature of everyone and mentally speak to them with conviction:

> I acknowledge your innate, divine nature.
> I see you in God.
> I see you spiritually enlightened.
> I see you whole.
> I see you fulfilled in every way.

Rest for a few minutes in peaceful awareness of oneness. Be thankful.

I do not have exceptional experiences or insights when I meditate. Should I continue to practice?

Practice regularly and you will become more proficient. Relax into meditation. Insights will occur randomly when you are not meditating. As understanding of your true nature in relationship with God improves and you are able to live more effectively, you can be sure that you are making progress.

Regular practice of meditation to the stage of deep relaxation, mental calmness, and clarity of awareness provides these constructive benefits:

- The body's immune system is strengthened.
- Biologic aging processes are slowed.
- Regenerative influences are activated.
- The nervous system is refined.

- The brain functions more effectively.
- After meditation, thinking is more rational.
- Intellectual and intuitive powers improve.
- Powers of concentration improve.
- Appreciation for living is enhanced.
- Spiritual growth can occur more easily.

Brain scans reveal that the prefrontal lobes of the brain—related to creativity, powers of concentration, discernment, and the ability to make wise choices—are involved during deep meditation and become more developed when meditation is regularly practiced. Harmonious interactions between the two hemispheres of the brain are also more evident in meditators.

How can we discern the difference between meditative perceptions and sensations that are mind- or brain-produced and authentic superconscious perceptions?

Subjective perceptions of light, sound, ecstatic feelings, and other phenomena produced by the mind and/or brain may be erroneously thought to be evidence that one is experiencing a superconscious state. Continue to meditate until a calm, clear state of awareness prevails that is devoid of subjective phenomena.

Is a vegetarian diet necessary for a person who is on a spiritual path?

A vegetarian diet is healthier, and is evidence of sincerity about being as harmless as possible in thought and deed. Adhere to orderly, wholesome lifestyle regimens that will contribute to good health. Healthy, long life enables us to more easily accomplish all of our useful purposes, including awakening to Self- and God-realization.

Because of my family and job-related duties and responsibilities, it is difficult for me to study metaphysical principles and meditate as often as I would like to. What should I do?

Schedule at least one hour a day to do this. You will be happier and be able to perform duties more easily and skillfully. At all times, be aware that you are a spiritual being living in the ocean of Infinite Life. Conscious, attentive performance of duties is also spiritual practice.

I think I would be more focused and inspired if I had someone with whom to share my ideals and to encourage me.

While spiritual friendships can be enjoyable, it is more important to nurture your will to accomplish your aims in life. You have the potential to be successful. Be Self-motivated.

I tend to be easily distracted by events in my life and the words and behaviors of others. What can I do to be more focused?

View events with dispassionate objectivity. Be so Self-aware that what others say or do will not disturb your inner peace or cause you to waver from your meaningful aims in life.

One of the results of early morning meditation and inspirational reading is that it will anchor your life in the Infinite and enable you to think and act more wisely. If stress or confusion has been accumulated during your daily activities, meditate a few minutes in the early evening to unstress your nervous system and quiet your mind and emotions.

I have several times made a commitment to the spiritual path and several times have weakened in my resolve. What can I do to persist in the right way? Also, I am afraid of dying.

Regularly read or listen to truth teachings to be inspired and motivated. Establish and adhere to wholesome lifestyle regimens and effective spiritual practices. Live with a sense of purpose that is of value to you.

I do not know anyone who cheerfully and with confidence anticipates their eventual transition from the body. Through the ages, many people have talked or written about how to prepare for that event. While it is easy for others to tell us what they think and what to do, we will have to confront that moment in our own way. The best preparation for your future well-being is to live with conscious intention now.

Most people do not remember their birth into this world nor their circumstances preceding this incarnation. We came here from inner space and to it we shall eventually return. While we are here, we have opportunities to learn all that we possibly can, cultivate and use our creative abilities, and complete our spiritual awakening.

Make the most of opportunities that you have while you are inspired. As the orderly processes of life have provided for you until now, they, and God's grace, will continue to do so. Be realistic, practical, and skillful in all that you do while having utmost faith in the goodness of life.

Can fantasy be used constructively?

While unmonitored fantasy is not beneficial, it can be useful to allow your imagination to roam freely when first beginning to think about what may be possible for you to accomplish. Doing this can enable you to rise above thoughts or feelings of limitation and bring forth useful ideas. Then progress to specific imagining of circumstances that will be of value to you.

As I get older, the years seem to be passing quickly and I often wonder if I will accomplish my aim of being Self- and God-realized before I leave this world. What should I do?

Stay on a meaningful course of right living, metaphysical study, and meditation practice. Expect to be spiritually awake. We do not know when a gradual, or sudden, shift of viewpoint will occur that will enable us to actually experience the truth of what we are and the reality of God.

To the often asked question, "How will I know

when I am Self- and God-realized?", the only answer is: When you are, you will know it. In the meantime, you should notice that your ability to live effectively and to comprehend the facts of life is progressively improving and all aspects of your life are better. View your life and your learning and growing opportunities as a great adventure.

Many people can only imagine what their life can, or might, be like within the boundaries of one incarnation and think and live in accord with that limited vision of possibilities. Expand your awareness and see far beyond existing circumstances to what can be true for you.

What is an effective way to overcome addictive thinking and behaviors?

Compulsive or obsessive attachments to any self-limiting habit of thinking or behavior can be overcome by choice and constructive actions. Behaviors that provide a temporary sense of pleasure or well-being are enacted in an attempt to provide a substitute for the joyous well-being that would be naturally experienced if one were Self-aware and at peace with themselves and the world. Destructive behaviors are symptoms of self-dislike along with thoughts and feelings of unworthiness and a conscious or unconscious inclination to be punished.

The permanent cure for all addictions is Self-knowledge that enables one to be willing to grow to emotional maturity.

I need physical healing and I need to be more prosperous. Are some problems caused by karma that was created in a previous incarnation and have to be endured?

Discover the causes of problems and eliminate them. To affirm that limiting circumstances are related to a previous incarnation is a convenient way of avoiding responsibility for confronting and overcoming them. Accept the fact that you can and will be healed. Bring forth your innate healing powers. Adopt a wholesome lifestyle. Cultivate optimism and a cheerful mental attitude. Refuse to believe in or claim misfortune or limitation. Claim vital health and total freedom to express. Think and act as a freely functional spiritual being.

I do not have satisfying results when I meditate. I try a variety of methods and really "work at it."

You *can* have satisfying results. Don't "work at" meditation practice; relax into it. Use a useful method to calm the mind, then sit in silence, aware of the essence of your being as pure consciousness. Continue to sit until your awareness is clear and you feel (at the core of your being) whole. Avoid anxiety about the results of practice. Sit on a daily schedule and let the results be what they will. At other times, established in Self-awareness and an intuitive sense of being one with the Infinite, live with conscious intention.

How can I overcome my feelings of loneliness? I have

a few friends, but there is no one with whom I feel a strong bond.

The only lasting cure for loneliness is Self-knowledge and emotional maturity. You will then be able to enjoyably relate to others without having any thoughts or feelings of need. Be supportive of others without wanting or needing anything in return. If thoughts or feelings of loneliness arise, avoid dwelling on them: do something constructive that will elicit positive thoughts and feelings. When you feel sad or lonely, physical exercise can be helpful because it causes the brain to secrete chemicals that produce feelings of well-being.

I have heard that some people who are believed to be spiritually enlightened say that troubles and hardships are to be accepted as "God's will" for us; that they can teach us valuable lessons.

God does not cause our troubles and hardships. Conditions that exist have mental, emotional, physical, or environmental causes that can be found and eliminated. Everyone should know this, and should not believe or say that God is capable of causing misfortune.

Can I really be Self-realized during my present incarnation?

Self-realization is possible at any moment. Awakening to it should not be thought of as being related to time or external conditions.

How can we know what is for our highest good?

Whatever enhances our lives and contributes to increased clarity of awareness and improved understanding of our true nature and God is for our highest good. Conditions which enhance our lives are good health; peace of mind; emotional stability and maturity; wholesome, supportive personal relationships; financial resources as needed; secure environmental circumstances; and opportunities to freely express, learn, and fulfill our potential for spiritual awakening.

While you are in this world you can be fulfilled and freely expressive while you are nurturing your spiritual growth. It is a mistake to concentrate only on spiritual growth and ignore or minimize the importance of balanced living. As your powers of perception and abilities to function improve, wisely use them to enhance your life and the lives of others.

Train yourself to think rationally and to be optimistic, emotionally stable, and to perform all actions with alert intention. Doing this is the best spiritual training. Do what you know is best for your total well-being, with your spiritual well-being first in order of importance.

Don't allow whims, sentiment, the opinions of others, or circumstances to control your thoughts, feelings, or actions. As a dedicated disciple on the spiritual path, you do not want to be ordinary; you want to be soul- and God-aware at all times.

How concerned should I be about my karma in relationship to my potential to be Self-realized?

Three categories of karma (subconscious and unconscious conditionings) may prevail until the mind is purified:

1) influences that are now evident.
2) influences that may be activated at any time.
3) latent impressions that may be influential in the future.

Constructive subconscious influences can be allowed to prevail if their effects enhance our lives. Troublesome influences should be resisted and overcome by positive thinking and actions.

Influences that may be easily activated can be resisted and weakened by constructive thinking and actions and cultivating mental and emotional calmness and stability.

The potency of latent subliminal impressions can be resisted, weakened, and neutralized by superconscious influences which purify both the mind and the body.

When the first two categories of subconscious influences are neutralized and Self-realization is constant, we are "liberated while embodied." When latent impressions are neutralized, our consciousness is completely liberated.

Do we have free will? Or are our experiences, including spiritual awakenings, predestined?

If we did not have free will, we would be unable

to choose our thoughts and actions. We have free will in regard to how we choose to live. We are predestined to sooner or later awaken through the stages of spiritual growth until we are Self- and God-realized. Although we may consciously or unconsciously resist the fulfillment of our destiny, we cannot avoid the final outcome. The awareness of all souls that are involved with mundane conditions will eventually be restored to purity.

Some spiritual teachers stress the importance of detachment. How can we live in this world without some attachments?

What is meant is to perform duties and relate to others without being dependent or mentally or emotionally disturbed by what occurs. The ideal is to be Self- and God-centered while engaged in useful activities and meaningful relationships.

Affirmation

The enlivening Spirit of God is freely expressive in, through, and around me. It illumines my mind, clarifies my awareness, inspires me with creative ideas, harmoniously arranges all of my circumstances and relationships in divine order for my highest good, and liberates my consciousness.

Center for Spiritual Awareness

Our international headquarters is located in the northeast Georgia mountains, 90 miles north of Atlanta. Facilities include our offices and CSA Press book publishing department, the Shrine of All Faiths Meditation Temple, the Meeting Hall and dining room, six guest houses, two library buildings, and a bookstore.

Weekend and week long meditation retreats are offered on a donation basis from spring until late autumn. Vegetarian meals are served when retreats are in session.

Truth Journal is published quarterly. Printed lessons are mailed each month to our international membership. *Radiance* magazine is published quarterly for kriya yoga initiates.

A 501(c)(3) nonprofit organization.

*A free literature packet and
book list may be requested.*

Center for Spiritual Awareness
P.O. Box 7
Lakemont, Georgia 30552-0001

Tel: 706-782-4723 Fax: 706-782-4560
e-mail: csainc@csa-davis.org
Internet Web Site: www.csa-davis.org